GET INTO CLAYMATION

KELLY SPENCE

CRABTREE
Publishing Company
www.crabtreebooks.com

Author: Kelly Spence

Editors: Marcia Abramson, Philip Gebhardt

Photo research: Melissa McClellan

Editorial director: Kathy Middleton

Proofreader: Janine Deschenes

Cover/Interior Design: T.J. Choleva

Production coordinator and
   Prepress technician: Samara Parent

Print coordinator: Margaret Amy Salter

Consultant: Sarah Hodgson
Art, Animation and New Media teacher,
Hamilton-Wentworth District School Board

Developed and produced for Crabtree Publishing
by BlueApple*Works* Inc.

Project Designers

Diorama on page 22 – Joshua Avramson; diorama on page 24 – Melissa McClellan; models on pages 26, 28 – Janet Compare-Fritz

Photographs

Shutterstock.com: © Lenor Ko (cover top banner); © RoyStudioEU (p. 5 bottom background); © colors (p. 4, 5, 22, 24, 26, 28 yellow background); © Valentina Razumova (p. 6 bottom left);

© Photofest: p. 5 top right, p.5 bottom right;

© Austen Photography: front cover, title page,TOC, p. 4, 8, 9, 10, 11, 12, 13, 14, 15, 16, 17, 18, 19, 20, 21, 24, 25, 26, 27, 28, 29, 31, 32;

© Janet Kompare-Fritz p. 7;

© Sam Taylor (p 10 bottom left);

© Molly Klager: front cover, p. 19 right, back cover

Library and Archives Canada Cataloguing in Publication

Spence, Kelly, author
        Get into claymation / Kelly Spence.

(Get-into-it guides)
Includes index.
Issued in print and electronic formats.
ISBN 978-0-7787-3400-0 (hardcover).—
ISBN 978-0-7787-3404-8 (softcover).--
ISBN 978-1-4271-1913-1 (HTML)

        1. Animation (Cinematography)--Juvenile literature. 2. Clay animation
films--Juvenile literature. I. Title.

TR897.6.S64 2017   j777'.7   C2016-907382-3
                                           C2016-907383-1

Library of Congress Cataloging-in-Publication Data

Names: Spence, Kelly, author.
Title: Get into claymation / Kelly Spence.
Description: New York, New York : Crabtree Publishing Company, [2017] | Series: Get-into-it guides | Includes index.
Identifiers: LCCN 2017000082 (print) | LCCN 2017000850 (ebook) | ISBN 9780778734000 (reinforced library binding : alk. paper) | ISBN 9780778734048 (pbk. : alk. paper) | ISBN 9781427119131 (Electronic HTML)
Subjects: LCSH: Animation (Cinematography)--Juvenile literature. | Clay animation films--Juvenile literature.
Classification: LCC TR897.6 .S64 2017 (print) | LCC TR897.6 (ebook) | DDC 777/.7--dc23
LC record available at https://lccn.loc.gov/2017000082

Crabtree Publishing Company

www.crabtreebooks.com   1-800-387-7650

Printed in Canada/032017/BF20170111

Published in Canada
Crabtree Publishing
616 Welland Ave.
St. Catharines, Ontario
L2M 5V6

Published in the United States
Crabtree Publishing
PMB 59051
350 Fifth Avenue, 59th Floor
New York, New York 10118

Published in the United Kingdom
Crabtree Publishing
Maritime House
Basin Road North, Hove
BN41 1WR

Published in Australia
Crabtree Publishing
3 Charles Street
Coburg North
VIC, 3058

CONTENTS

STOP-MOTION ANIMATION

Stop-motion **animation** is a filmmaking technique in which still, or unmoving, pictures are played in rapid sequence to create the impression of movement. Rapid sequence means that the images are played very quickly in a specific order. Each image is called a **frame**. Each frame shows a small change in position from the previous frame.

Claymation, also known as clay animation, uses stop-motion techniques to create movies starring puppets made out of modeling clay. Modeling clay is used because it is easy to work with. It allows **animators** to easily move and reposition the puppets in tiny steps to show movement. Claymation requires patience and attention to detail. It takes hundreds of frames to make a Claymation movie. Animations can be created using many devices, including a traditional camera, smartphone, tablet, or webcam.

Claymation movies are usually shorter than other movies because they require more work.

How To Use This Book

The projects in this book are meant to inspire you to create your own Claymation movies. You can follow the steps provided, or use your imagination to add your own creative twists to the projects.

4

BECOMING AN ANIMATOR

A career in animation requires hard work. You can gain experience by joining clubs or entering contests. Many schools and libraries hold workshops to teach animation techniques. With a responsible adult's permission, you can also watch how-to videos online. Observe your surroundings and keep a notebook to jot down ideas. You never know when inspiration will hit! At college, animators might study sculpture, animation, or illustration. The only limit to making Claymation movie magic is your imagination.

Did You Know?

*In 1955, well-known Claymation characters Gumby and his trusty horse Pokey were brought to life by animator Art Clokey (1921–2010). The characters appeared in a popular TV series, and even starred in a movie. In 2015, to celebrate Gumby's 60th birthday, Gumby Fest, a stop-motion animation festival, was held at Citrus College in California. The festival included an exhibition that featured the original puppets, **props**, and **sets** from the hit TV show.*

CLAYMATION MASTERPIECES

Clay animation got its start way back in 1897 when modeling clay was invented. During the 1960s, characters such as Gumby became popular. The first Claymation feature film was *Chicken Run*, released in 2000. The creators spent two and a half years planning the story and making the puppets, then a year and a half shooting the movie. To shoot 10 seconds of film, about 240 frames were needed. During filming, 7,000 pounds (3,175 kg) of Plasticine, a type of modeling clay, was used. More than 500 puppets were made. All the hard work paid off—*Chicken Run* is the **top-grossing** Claymation movie of all time. Other feature-length Claymation movies include *The Curse of the Were-Rabbit* (2005), *The Pirates! Band of Misfits* (2012), and *Shaun the Sheep Movie* (2015).

It takes a lot of time to shoot a Claymation movie. About 10–12 frames are needed for one second of film. It took five years to shoot The Curse of the Were-Rabbit!

CLAYMATION MAGIC

It takes imagination, planning, and lots of work to achieve the magical look of Claymation. The first thing you need is a good story. Jot down your ideas and choose the one you like best. Now write out the full **story line**. Make sure your story moves along clearly from the start to the conclusion. Once you have the story line finished, create a **storyboard** that shows how to set up each frame.

Now you are ready to make your puppets, build sets, and create props. Gather all your materials before you start working with clay. You also need to choose which camera and software (see below) to use.

Make sure you have a steady, bright light to shine on your set. When you have put the set, light, and camera in position, you are ready to make movie magic, one frame at a time. It's important to remember that each time you make a change in the scene, no matter how small, you need to take a new photo. When you have all your pictures, use software to assemble your frames into a movie.

ANIMATION SOFTWARE

There are many stop-motion software programs and **applications** (apps) available for animators of all skill levels, from a beginner to a professional. Be sure to check with an adult before downloading any apps or software to your device. Some programs allow you to shoot your frames directly in the program, then string them together. Others require you to upload the pictures from your camera. Most programs feature a **tutorial** that teaches filmmakers how to use the different tools.

HOW IT WORKS

You will need to learn how your software operates, but most stop-motion programs work something like this:

1. *The software displays all the frames from the camera on-screen as thumbnails, or small pictures.*
2. *The animator clicks on a single thumbnail to select it. This step is repeated as many times as necessary and in the right order.*
3. *When all the frames have been selected, the animator previews what the movie will look like and makes changes if needed.*
4. *When everything looks good, the animator uses the program to combine all the frames into one file. It's now ready for music, **credits**, and other additions.*

PLANNING YOUR VIDEO - STORYBOARDS

A storyboard is a tool animators use to plan the different scenes that will be included in a movie. It shows what will happen, and in what order. Each frame is sketched to show the position of the puppets. A storyboard also shows the kind of shot, such as a close-up, being used in each frame. Make a storyboard to plan the action in your Claymation. For now, focus on showing large changes instead of small movements. Try using different shots to create suspense or add humor. Draw in pencil in case you want to make changes.

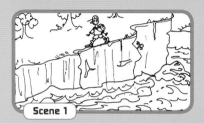
Scene 1

Scene 2

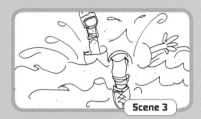
Scene 3

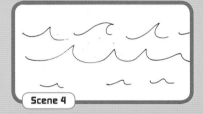
Scene 4

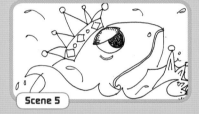
Scene 5

Scene 6

A storyboard showing six frames.

EDITING YOUR MOVIE

Editing is the process of reviewing your work and making changes. Clay animators often reuse frames that show a repeated movement, such as walking. They can use the same picture twice in a row to cut down on the number of frames needed. At other times, frames can be reversed to show characters moving backward or walking around in circles. Pauses are important, too. Create a pause by repeating a single frame several times. Experiment with reusing frames to find interesting ways to enhance your movie while saving time shooting the frames. You can also add music and sound at the editing stage to bring your movie to life. Animation programs and apps usually come pre-loaded with lots of music and sound effects. You can also record your own sounds or a **dialogue** between your characters. Include the title of your movie at the beginning of your finished Claymation. Add credits at the end to **acknowledge** everyone who worked on it. Finally, set up a **screening** to show your finished product to an audience!

Tip

Use music to create a soundtrack for your movie. Think about how you can match the music to the mood of your characters. Are they happy or sad, silly or scared? You could even create a movie based on a simple song or nursery rhyme.

SHOOTING AND LIGHTING

Along with the movement of the puppets, animators use different shots and lighting to show progression in their movies. Remember, the smaller the movements, the smoother the **transition** will appear in your finished animation. Try to keep your lighting consistent, too.

To film a 30-minute short movie, the animators who created *Wallace and Gromit* shot 20 frames per second (fps). The entire movie required about 36,000 frames! For your animation, start by shooting 10–12 fps. For a faster scene, you may need more. For a slower scene, you can use less.

THE CREW

It takes a lot of work to put together a Claymation movie. Working in a group is a fun way to get it all done. Assign a different role to each person. One person can position the puppets, while another snaps the pictures. When you are taking pictures, make sure everyone's hands are not in the frame. If a hand or finger is included by accident, you can remove it at the editing stage.

BREAKS AND PAUSES

*Building breaks and pauses into your movie will make it feel more natural and **authentic**. To create a pause, repeat a single frame six or more times or extend the length of one frame. Your audience needs at least a few seconds to register the pause.*

LIGHT IT UP

Consistent, controlled lighting is important when shooting a Claymation movie. Using a few desk lamps that are easy to position will work great to light your set. You can also light your set from above with overhead lights or a tall lamp. It's better to stay indoors and to avoid using light from a window because natural light is always changing, which will cause flickering in your frames.

Set up your lights, then snap a few test shots. Make adjustments as needed until you are happy with the look.

Flat, even light is created by placing two lamps an equal distance apart. There are few or no shadows.

A spotlight from a flashlight can keep the focus on a specific part of the set.

CAMERAS

You can use any camera that can capture digital images to shoot your Claymation. It is very important to keep the camera still while you are taking pictures. Using a **tripod** helps hold the camera steady and in the correct position. If you do not have a tripod, try setting your camera on a stack of books to keep it at the same height.

It is a good idea to position the camera at least 3 feet (91 cm) away from your scene to avoid having to move the camera for different shots. Zoom out so that you can see the entire set through the camera lens. Then zoom in to shoot close-up shots.

An **establishing shot** shows the entire set. It's a good way to set up a scene.

A close-up can show facial expressions and lots of detail.

Shooting a scene from above makes the character look smaller.

A low shot can make a puppet appear bigger or more powerful.

CHECKING POSITIONS

Onion skinning is a feature that allows animators to see how frames blend together. Included in some animation programs, it shows a **transparent** image of the previous frame. By using this tool, you can see how a character is positioned in relation to the previous frame. Onion skinning can help you determine the best position for your puppet to create a smooth, seamless motion. The tool also comes in handy if you need to reposition a puppet that has fallen over.

Here is an example of onion skinning. It shows the character's changed position from one frame to the next.

Tip

You can shoot your Claymation near a light source controlled by a dimmer switch to create a sunrise or sunset effect.

LIGHTING EFFECTS

Flashlights can be used to create mood lighting in your movie. Think of creative ways you can use the light in your story. In a science-fiction movie, you could use a flashlight to beam your character up into a spaceship. You can also cover a flashlight with different colors of cellophane or tissue paper. Use red, orange, or yellow to create a fiery sunset scene, and blue and green for a space or evening effect.

CREATING YOUR CHARACTERS

It is time to design your puppets based on your storyboard. To show movement, you need to be able to change the position of your puppets. It is important to use a nondrying clay, such as Plasticine. If you do not use a nondrying clay, your puppets will harden and crack when repositioned. Although they can appear life-size in some movies, puppets are usually about the size of an action figure, 4 to 8 inches (10 to 20 cm) tall. They should be big enough to move around, but not so big that they fall over. That way, they are easier to position.

WORKING WITH STYROFOAM SHAPES

If a puppet is too heavy, it might start to droop while you are shooting your frames. Styrofoam shapes can keep puppets lightweight, and also reduce the amount of clay you need.

1 Buy an assortment of Styrofoam shapes at a craft or dollar store.

2 Use a thin layer of clay to completely cover the foam.

3 Use your fingers to smooth out the clay.

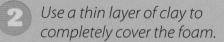

4 Attach the arms and legs to the body. Give your puppet wide, flat feet to help it stand on its own.

Tip

It's a good idea to start with simple figures that are easy to make. As you gain more experience working with clay, you can add lots of cool and interesting details.

WORKING WITH CLAY

Nondrying clay can be messy to work with. Cover your work station with a plastic tablecloth or a flat piece of cardboard. Wear old clothes or an apron. Roll and **knead** a ball of clay in your hands to soften it. This makes it easier to work with. If you are using different colors of clay, make all the pieces that are the same color first. This keeps the colors from mixing together. When you are done, clean up your materials and wash your hands well with soap and water.

CRAFTING ARMATURES

Some puppets can be animated by simply bending or molding the clay. For more complicated or larger puppets, many animators use **armatures**. An armature is a frame inside the puppet. It provides support like a skeleton, allowing you to bend and position the different parts of the puppet. It is often used together with Styrofoam, which usually makes up the bigger parts of the puppet. Flexible, lightweight wire, such as aluminum craft wire, works well. Once your armature is complete, cover it with a layer of nondrying clay.

You will need about a 40-inch (100-cm) long wire to make an armature for a 6-inch (15-cm) puppet. Adjust the length of wire as needed for bigger or smaller puppets.

1 *Cut a long piece of wire. Bend it in half, then twist the two pieces together two or three times near the top, leaving a small loop for the head.*

2 *To make an arm, bend a short length of wire just below the twist. Leaving a small loop for the hand, coil the wire back on itself. Use the same steps to make a second arm on the other side.*

4 *Gently press a Styrofoam ball onto the top loop for the puppet's head. Do not press too hard or the foam will crack.*

3 *For the body, twist the two loose pieces of wire together, about the same length as an arm. Make two legs using the arm technique.*

USING MOUTH SHAPES

Mouth shapes can show a puppet's emotions, and can be animated to show a change. A circular mouth can be easily repositioned to show changes, such as the ones below.

Gloomy Expression
Show that your character is sad with a closed mouth that is curved downward.

Shocked Expression
An open, circular mouth shows astonishment and shock.

Happy Expression
Give your puppet a friendly smile by pointing the corners of its mouth upward.

Gross Expression
A straight, mostly closed mouth shows viewers that a character is grossed out.

HUMAN FIGURES

Creating human figures can be challenging. Remember to keep your puppets to **scale** so they fit with your set and props. They need to be strong and stable. Big feet or a big base will help support **3-D** puppets, and putty or pushpins can be used to anchor them, or keep them in place. Magnets are used to anchor **2-D** puppets.

CREATING TWO-DIMENSIONAL HIKER WITH A MAGNET

This character will be used in the movie project on pages 26–27. This puppet is flat on one side. During animation, only one side will be visible. Following the steps below will help you to create many other 2-D characters.

1 *Flatten a large piece of clay on your work station. Use your hands or a rolling pin to press the clay into a smooth slab, about 1/4 inch (1 cm) thick.*

2 *With a modeling tool or wooden skewer, draw an outline of your hiker. Use a plastic knife to cut out your shape. Remove the extra clay.*

3 *Break a toothpick or wooden skewer into pieces that fit the size of the hiker.*

4 *Press the pieces onto the back of the puppet to give it extra support.*

5 *Press clay on top of the sticks to hold them in place. Gently press a magnet into the puppet's back.*

6 *Use small pieces of colored clay to decorate your hiker. Add details such as an eye, a hat, and hiking boots.*

CREATING A SKATEBOARDER FIGURE

This 3-D skateboarder will be used in the movie project on pages 24–25. An armature and a foam ball are used to build this character to help make it light and sturdy. This technique can be used to build many different figures.

pages 24–25

1 Make an armature following the steps shown on page 11.

2 For the puppet's head, gently press a foam ball onto the top loop of the armature.

3 Cover the armature with a layer of clay. Leave the feet uncovered. Add more clay to build up the puppet's body. Form hands at the end of the arms.

4 Roll two clay ovals, then gently flatten them. Press each wire foot into the oval, then add more clay to cover the wire.

5 Use blue clay to cover each shoe. Add thin strips of black clay for shoelaces.

6 Cover each arm with white clay. Add a thin strip of white clay around the puppet's neck. Then make a red T-shirt with a thin layer of clay. Wrap black clay around the lower torso and legs to make pants.

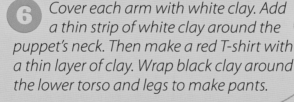

7 Add extra clay for a nose. Stick googly eyes onto the face, and draw a mouth with a modeling tool. Use bits of brown clay for your puppet's hair.

8 Safety first! Add a helmet, elbow pads, and knee pads to your puppet. Make straps using thin strips.

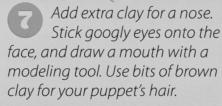

9 Make a skateboard for your puppet to ride (see page 16).

ANIMAL FIGURES

Think about ways you can use animals in a Claymation. You could shoot a step-by-step transformation, such as a caterpillar emerging from a cocoon as a butterfly or a chick hatching from an egg. You could create an adventure with a dragon soaring through the sky. You can also use human and animal puppets together in a Claymation.

CREATING THE FROG CHARACTER

This character will be used in the movie project on pages 26-27. An armature is not needed because the puppet is bulky and short. However, you could use a foam ball for its body to reduce the amount of clay needed.

1 *Make an oval shape for the body. Shape a large ball of clay in your hands, then roll it against a flat surface to smooth it.*

2 *Use your fingers to pinch and roll one end into a head shape.*

3 *Make four legs by dividing another large piece of clay into four pieces. Roll each piece in your hand, then roll it on a flat surface to smooth it.*

4 *Press the legs into the body and shape them. (Look at a picture of a frog for guidance.) Flatten the clay at the end of each leg.*

5 *Add eyes and a mouth. You can also decorate the frog with small pieces of colored clay.*

6 *Place a crown on top of the frog's head. (See page 21 for instructions to make the crown.)*

The spider character will be used in the movie project on page 28-29. A wire armature and a foam ball will keep its long legs in place during animation.

The spider character will be used in the movie project on page 28-29.

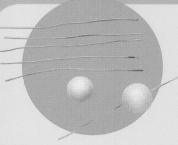

Tip
You could use a store-bought spider for your movies. They are inexpensive and usually look rather spooky. Just make sure that the size you pick matches your clay-made characters and other props.

1 Use five pieces of craft wire and a foam ball to make the armature. Push one piece of wire through the center of the ball as shown.

2 Push another piece of wire through the ball to make a squashed-looking X with the other wire, as shown.

3 Push two more pieces of wire through the ball as shown.

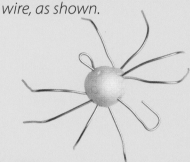

5 Push the last piece of wire through the ball as shown. Leave the ends slightly out at each end. Bend the end of each wire into a hook shape using pliers.

6 Make a head using a small ball of clay. Press the head onto the front hook to attach it to the wire.

4 Bend the wires into leg shapes.

8 Decorate the spider with different colors of clay or other accessories to make it scarier.

7 Carefully cover the body and legs with a thin layer of black or brown clay. Leave the hook in the back uncovered. It will be used to hold the spider in place.

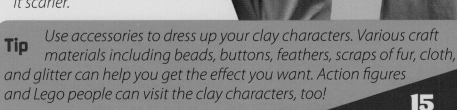

Tip Use accessories to dress up your clay characters. Various craft materials including beads, buttons, feathers, scraps of fur, cloth, and glitter can help you get the effect you want. Action figures and Lego people can visit the clay characters, too!

MAKING THEM MOVE

The magic of stop-motion animation is creating the illusion of movement. There are many ways to move the characters on the set. There are times when animators have to come up with unique setups to achieve their animation goals. Keep it simple at first. Once you understand the process of creating Claymation and stop-motion movies, you can try to perfect your techniques and learn some tricks!

USING WHEELS

Create moving bases for your characters using old toy cars and other wheeled toys. This technique can come in handy when shooting a sports Claymation.

To make a skateboard, cover a small toy car with clay. Do not put clay on the wheels. Cut a skateboard out of cardboard and cover it with a layer of clay. Press the skateboard down on top of the car. You can add fake wheels to the sides of the skateboard, but make sure they do not stop the spinning motion of the toy car wheels.

Tip

Over time, your puppets might start to develop cracks or show fingerprints. If that happens, gently rub the puppet's surface with your fingers to smooth out the clay. It is also a good idea to keep your fingernails short so they do not mark the clay.

MORPHING TECHNIQUE

Morphing clay is a simple way to make a clay figure change shape. It is a great way to learn and test your animation skills.

Place a blob of clay on your set. Take a picture.

Pinch the blob slightly in the middle. Take another picture.

Continue pinching the clay in small steps and taking pictures until you have created a whole new shape.

FLYING AND FALLING

Magnets can be used to make 2-D puppets appear to move along the back of your set. When the magnets connect, they hold the figure in place. You can animate the figure by moving it up, down, or side to side.

Tip

Make sure that your magnets are set up properly. The two ends or sides of a magnet are called the north and south poles. A north pole will attract a south pole, and the magnets will stick together. If you put a north pole next to a north pole, magnets will repel each other. If that happens, turn one magnet over and try again.

You will need two magnets. Gently press one into the back of your figure. Bar magnets work best, but circular magnets can work too.

Hold your puppet on the front of your set against the background. Line up a second magnet behind the paper.

The two magnets will attract, holding your puppet in place. If your puppet is too heavy, add an extra set of magnets.

DISAPPEARING EFFECT

What if you want to make your character disappear? One easy way to achieve this effect is by slicing off tiny portions from the bottom of your character between frames.

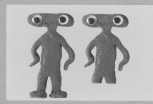

Lay the puppet flat on a table. Use a plastic knife to cut a thin layer of clay off the bottom.

Place the character back on the set. Make sure it is placed in the same angle and location on the set as it was in the previous shot.

Keep repeating this process and taking pictures in sequence. Repeat until the character disappears from the scene.

THE BLINK OF AN EYE

To make your puppet blink, prepare two thin circles and half-circles of clay.

Place the half-circles on the eyes. Take a picture.

Place the full circles on the eyes. Take a picture.

Place the half-circles on the eyes again and take the picture. Finally, remove the half-circles.

BUILDING SETS

A set is the place where you will shoot your Claymation movie. All you need is a surface on which to position your puppets, but adding details to a set will help bring your Claymation to life. If you are shooting a spooky shot, why not create a graveyard? For an underwater adventure, you can build a set that looks like the ocean floor. You can use paint, felt, or other materials to decorate.

If you choose to create a realistic set, do some research. To create an African grassland, look at pictures on the Internet or in books. You could also use a student **diorama** as an instant set.

BASIC SET

For a simple backdrop, use a large sheet of paper or poster board. Tape one end to the wall, then tape the other to a flat surface. The paper will curve slightly.

CARDBOARD SET

1 *Use a cardboard box to make a set. Take the box apart and cut out the two longer sides. They should be the same size.*

2 *Attach the two pieces with masking tape as shown.*

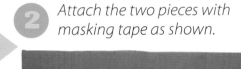

3 *Cut a triangle out of the leftover cardboard.*

4 *Bend the cardboard into an L-shape. Tape the triangle to the upright piece to hold it up.*

5 *Cover the front of the set with a sheet of colored paper. Tape or glue it in place. Blue can be used for the sky.*

Hot Set

A director oversees the production of a movie. When he or she calls a set "hot," this lets the crew know that nothing can be touched, including the props and puppets. This is especially important in stop-motion, in which details are very important.

PIZZA BOX SET FOR USE WITH MAGNETS

A pizza box set is a great tool to animate objects in the sky, such as the Sun, Moon, and clouds. Use magnets to hold your props in place. To show time passing, clouds can float slowly across the sky in the background of your Claymation.

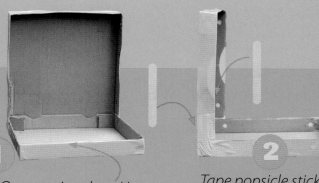

1 *Open a pizza box. Use tape to strengthen the box.*

2 *Tape popsicle sticks to the corners to hold the lid open.*

3 *Mark a square about 1 inch (2.5 cm) from the sides of the lid. Ask an adult to cut it out.*

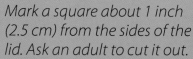

4 *Cut a piece of cardstock to fit the lid and tape or staple it to the pizza box frame. Cut off the front edge if you wish.*

6 *For the ground, choose a color that works best for your Claymation. Glue or tape it to the set.*

7 *Before you shoot a scene, arrange your props. Use putty or tape to secure them to the set.*

GREEN-SCREEN SETS

Green-screening is a technique that allows you to put any image in the background of your movie. The frames are shot against a green background that is later **keyed out** and replaced with the background of your choice. You can make your own green screen with a piece of green poster board, or a sheet of green fabric. When shooting your frames, position your puppets and props far enough away from the background so they do not cast shadows. Once you have all your frames, use a green-screen program to add in the background of your choice.

19

MAKING PROPS

Using your imagination and craft supplies, you can create props to decorate your set. You can also use toys and other small objects as long as they are on the same scale as your puppets and don't look too big or too small for the scene—unless that is the effect you are going for!

TREES AND SHRUBBERY

Make leaves by scrunching up small squares of tissue paper. Glue them onto the branches of the tree.

Bend a long piece of wire in half, then spread out the ends to make branches. Use a small ball of clay as a base. Press the wire into the base, then cover the wire with clay. Use a modeling tool to add details, such as bark or knots. Use moss or clay to make leaves. Make several trees to create a shady forest scene.

GRASS FEATURES

Fold a piece of green paper in half. Make small cuts with scissors along one edge to make grass.

To make grass using moss, use a flat strip of clay. Press the moss into the clay. Use larger pieces of moss to create bushes.

To make clay grass, mix together green and yellow clay. Press out a long, flat strip. Fold over one edge to make a wide base. Fringe the upright side with scissors or a plastic knife.

CLOUDS

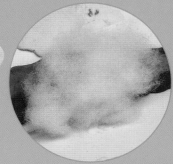

Clouds can be made by using flat, thin circles of clay. Use your fingers to pinch the edges to create a scalloped effect. For a stormy scene, use gray clay to make rain clouds.

Cotton balls or stuffing from an old toy can be used to create fluffy clouds. Cut a cloud shape out of white paper, then glue the stuffing on.

CROWN WITH CREST

Roll a small ball of clay. Break a toothpick to size. Insert it into the ball. Leave one end sticking out as shown. The stick will be used to attach the crown to the frog's head.

Press out a thin slab of yellow clay. Measure it to match the circumference of the ball, then cut out a rectangular shape as shown.

Cut out triangular sections from the clay strip and attach it to the ball as shown.

Cut out a cross-shaped **crest** from cardstock as shown and insert it into the top of the crown.

WATER FEATURES

Mix together different shades of blue clay to make water. Use a long, flat strip for a curving river. Form an oval for a pond or lake.

A strip of blue tissue or crepe paper can be used to make a river. Glue small stones, grass, or moss along the edges. Cut long, thin strips of paper to make rushing water. (Use strips of red and orange paper to make a river of fiery lava!)

SPOOKY STUFF

For a spooky scene, create a graveyard. Make a rectangular slab with gray clay. Round the corners to create a curved tombstone. Tombstones can also be cut out of cardboard and decorated with paint. Use clay or a marker to write names on the stones.

STONE-LIKE PROPS

Make 3-D cliffs using foamboard. Cut the shapes to fit your scene. Decorate them with paint. Once dry, position the pieces about 1 inch (2.5 cm) apart to create depth in your set.

WACKY TRANSFORMATION

Morphing is a special effect in motion pictures and animations that morphs, or changes, one image or shape into another seamlessly, or smoothly. Morphing can be used for many effects, from a simple blob of clay changing shape to more sophisticated transformations, such as a person turning into an animal. In this project, you will make a lump of clay morph into a happy character. This example is also a great way to create and use facial expressions to capture different moods.

Prepare your set and place the blob of clay in the center. As you start animating, make the blob shift from left to right to create a wobbling motion to show it is changing.

Pinch the clay where the shoulders will be and form short limbs. Frame by frame, show the blob's arms growing longer.

Animate the arms reaching toward the googly eyes. Then show the arms scooping the eyes up.

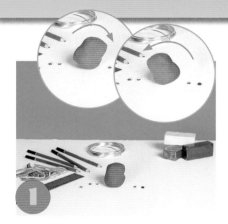

Add smile

Add sad expression

Bend back the arms. Show the blob placing the eyes on its "face," then rest the arms to its sides.

Animate the blob looking from left to right by turning it in both directions. Add a smiling mouth below the eyes. Turn the blob to the left and to the right several times again.

Show the blob looking down by bending its head down. Add a pause, then replace the smile with a sad expression.

Our Story Line:

In the opening scene, a blob of clay is sitting next to two googly eyes. The set looks like a modeling board with a few items left out by the animator who has left for the day. After a few seconds, the blob wobbles and begins to grow arms. It then reaches its arms out to explore its surroundings. It discovers the googly eyes, and puts them on to look around. A big smile appears on its face because it can see! Then it looks down and its smile changes to a sad expression. The blob wonders where its legs are. It wobbles again, and begins to morph. It starts to grow legs. The morph continues until it becomes a human-like figure. Clothes, hair, and ears appear next. The new character looks surprised, then breaks into a big, happy smile to end the scene.

Show the blob lift its head. Add a pause for a few seconds showing its sad face.

Create a wobbling motion like in step 1, to show that the blob will keep changing.

Pinch the clay at the bottom and form short limbs. Frame by frame, show the blob's legs growing longer.

 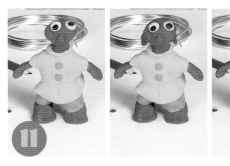 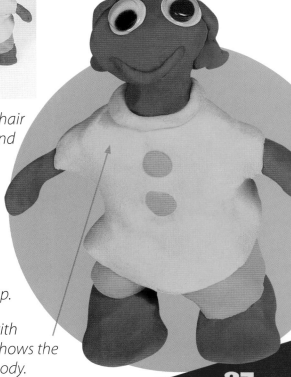

Pinch the clay in the middle and keep morphing it gradually until you form a human-shaped body.

Add clothes and take a picture. Then add hair and take another picture. Add ears next and take a picture. It is okay if it looks like everything happened suddenly without morphing.

Add surprised expression

12 *Bend the head down a little. Replace the sad expression with a surprised expression. Lift the head back up.*

13 *Replace the surprised expression with a happy expression. The last shot shows the newly formed blob happy with its new body.*

23

MOVIE PROJECT 2

ENERGIZER PAVILION

There are many ways to make your character move across the set. The simplest and most common way is to animate the character toward its destination in small steps. Adding wheels to your characters can also be helpful. Sometimes it fits with the theme of the scene. Other times, it just looks cool! In this project, wheels are used on a skateboarder figure to add to the contrast between super-slow and super-fast movements. The Energizer Pavilion will transform a slow character into a fast one. A pavilion is a large tent or tent-like building. You can use the pavilion concept to perform other changes, such as changing characters from little to big.

Prepare the set. Build a snail and place it on the left side of the platform. Take shots showing the snail move toward the pavilion.

Once the snail reaches the pavilion, move its antennae outward and then inward to show apprehension.

Shoot a sequence showing the door opening in small steps. Move the snail into the pavilion. Use your finger or a stick to push it all the way in.

Shoot a sequence showing the door closing in small steps.

Without taking pictures, open the pavilion and replace the snail figure with the skateboarder. Close the pavilion.

Move the top of the pavilion from side to side to show it shaking as the snail changes form. Do it several times, or duplicate the frames during the editing stage.

This project uses opposites to show a contrast. You can use this idea to highlight the difference between two objects, or to show a change. Think about ideas you can animate using this theme. For example, you could use this theme to illustrate the importance of proper nutrition and exercise versus unhealthy eating habits and lack of activity.

Our Story Line:

In the opening scene, a pavilion is set up in the middle of the set. A snail appears from the left, inching slowly toward the pavilion while slow, sad music plays. The snail enters the pavilion and the door closes behind it. The music changes to suspenseful. The pavilion shakes for several frames while transforming the snail. Suddenly, the door flies open. The music changes to a fast, energetic tune (a sound of a speeding engine would work here too) and out comes a skateboarder who quickly zooms away on her skateboard.

Begin the opening door sequence. Start pulling the door outward in small, quick steps.

Once the door is open, move the skateboarder out so she is visible in the doorway.

Show the skateboarder's head moving from side to side as if she is looking around.

Use the blinking technique from page 17 to make the skateboarder wink at the camera.

Shoot a series of frames showing the skateboarder zooming away from the pavilion.

If you want to keep it simple, do not change the skateboarder's position. For an extra challenge, reposition the skateboarder's arms so she appears to wave goodbye as she rolls away.

MOVIE PROJECT 3

CRESTFALLEN HIKER

Show off your Claymation skills by creating an animation of a puppet flying or falling! There are different ways to achieve this effect. You can tie clear fishing line to your puppet to suspend it in the air, or use magnets to create a falling-down motion on the background of your set. The magnet technique can be used on the background of a 3-D set, or you can create 2-D characters and props on a vertical background. Try securing a thin sheet of metal behind your background. This will make it easier to animate your puppets, as you will not need a second magnet to hold them in place.

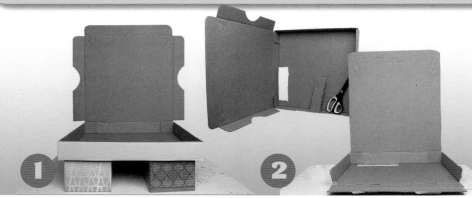

Use an empty pizza box for this set, or create your own set using cardstock for the background. Place the pizza box on supports about 4 inches (10 cm) in height.

Ask an adult to remove the front edge of the box and cut a slit in the bottom of the box next to the background. It needs to be big enough for your characters to fit through. Add the props.

Prepare your character by pressing a magnet into the back side of the hiker. Test the magnets to make sure they will hold the hiker on the set. Remove the hiker and add the props.

Position the camera at an angle that captures only the top of the set, not the supports and space below.

Position the hiker on the cliff. Start taking shots while moving the hiker toward the edge of the cliff.

Once the hiker reaches the edge, tilt him to the right and left to show him losing his balance. Next, have the hiker fall over toward the cliff.

This movie shows a fun way to create a theme using a play on words. The word "crestfallen" means being sad, depressed, or disheartened. It can be split into two words: "crest" and "fallen." In this movie, the character trips and falls into water, which is the play on "fallen." Then, in a twist on the fairy tale The Frog Prince, he emerges as a frog wearing a crown with a crest on it. And yes, he doesn't look very happy with the transformation, so he is "crestfallen." Try to think of other words you could use to create an animation with, or look one up in a dictionary to improve your vocabulary.

Our Story Line:

In the opening scene, a hiker Is shown standing on top of a cliff. The hiker takes a few steps toward the edge of the cliff, trips over a small rock, and falls into water below. The puppet disappears through the water level. A few seconds are shown with the hiker completely submerged to create suspense. Suddenly, a frog surfaces, wearing a crown with a crest. It looks around, then lifts its arms in disbelief. It has a sad facial expression, showing that it is "crestfallen."

7 Start shooting the falling-down sequence. Slowly show the puppet falling headfirst toward the water below.

8 Move the character through the slit in the bottom to create the submerging effect.

9 Once the character disappears from view, shoot several frames of empty set to create suspense. (In the editing stage, you can add an audio clip of crashing waves.)

10 Place the frog character under the set, lift it up, and in one quick move have it jump out of the water through the slit.

11 Turn the frog slightly to the left and to the right as if it's looking around.

12 Move the frog's arms upward. Attach a sad expression to the frog's face and have its arms come down to the surface.

13 Finish the movie showing the unhappy frog leaving the set. (In the editing stage, add a slow, sad audio clip that supports this effect.)

MOVIE PROJECT 4

HUNGRY HALLOWEEN SPIDER

Making characters appear and disappear adds fun and surprising elements to your Claymation. One easy way to achieve this effect is by slicing off tiny portions of your character in sequence and taking pictures of each change. The fun part is playing the disappearing sequence backward. Using this trick will make your character appear on your set as if out of thin air. Experiment with different playback speeds to find the right effect for your movie.

1 Prepare the set. Hook the spider onto the tree. (Optional: Use a red light bulb in one light, and a blue light bulb in the other to make spooky lighting.)

2 Build a zombie puppet and place it in the graveyard. Shoot some frames showing the zombie move toward the tree.

3 Once your zombie character reaches the tree, position the zombie so it turns to face the camera.

4 Start your spotlight lighting. Have a friend hold the spotlight on the spider in the tree.

5 Take shots showing the spider creeping down the tree toward the zombie. Use the hook to hold it in place for each step.

6 Remove the spider from the tree and attach it to the zombie's head. This sudden movement will create the impression of a jump when the sequence is played. Add a scream at the editing stage.

Our Story Line:

The opening scene shows a spooky graveyard. A tree stands in the middle of the set with a big black spider sitting in the branches. Spooky music plays. A zombie shuffles across the set, moving between tombstones. It stops under the tree, then turns toward the camera to look at the audience. The spider slowly creeps down the tree, jumps on the zombie, and starts to devour it. The zombie disappears, and the spider climbs back up the tree to rest, or wait for another snack. For an extra challenge, show a few more zombies in the background walking across the set.

Show the zombie struggling against the spider. Move the zombie slightly to the left and to the right to show it trying to escape.

Remove the zombie and spider from the set. Slice a piece of clay from the bottom of the zombie figurine.

Place the characters back on the set. Make sure they are exactly in the same spot and at the same angle as they were in the previous shot. Use the onion skinning feature explained on page 9 to help you, if possible.

Repeat steps 8 and 9 and keep shooting until only the zombie's head is visible.

Move the spider and the zombie's head sharply to the left and to the right as the spider finishes its supper. Remove the zombie's head from the set for the last shot. Remove the spotlight.

For the final sequence, show the spider returning to the tree to wait for another victim to walk by. (Add a suspenseful tune at the editing stage.)

29

LEARNING MORE

Books

Animation Studio
by Helen Piercy, Candlewick, 2013.

The Klutz Book of Animation
by John Cassidy and Nicholas Berger, Klutz, 2010.

The LEGO Animation Book: Make Your Own LEGO Movies!
by David Pagano and David Pickett, No Starch Press, 2016.

Maker Projects for Kids Who Love Animation
by Sarah Levete, Crabtree Publishing, 2016.

Monster Claymation
by Emily Reid, Windmill Books, 2016.

Movie Maker: The Ultimate Guide to Making Films
by Tim Grabham, Suridh Hassan, Dave Reeve, and Clare Richards,
Candlewick, 2010.

Websites

Aardman Animation's Animate It!
www.animate-it.com/category/get-animating/technical-tips/
Website includes videos on Claymation techniques from professional animators.

Maker Camp from *Make*: magazine
makezine.com/projects/clay-figures-for-claymation/
Create your own model of Shaun the Sheep following step-by-step instructions given
by British animators from Aardman Animations in this video.

Nick Park Interview
www.wallaceandgromit.com/nick-park
Watch an interview with animator Nick Park of Aardman Animations.

GLOSSARY

2-D Short for two-dimensional, having height and width; lacking the illusion of depth

3-D Short for three-dimensional, having height, length, and width, giving an illusion of depth

acknowledge To express thanks or appreciation for something or to someone

animation A movie made by taking pictures and playing them quickly in order to create movement

animators People who make animated movies, TV shows, or video games

app (application) A computer program that performs a particular task

armatures Frames that support figures or puppets that can be moved into different positions

authentic Real and accurate

credits Recognition given to people who worked together to make a movie or TV show

crest A decoration or a special symbol positioned on top of a crown to represent a specific family, group, or organization

dialogue A conversation between two or more people

diorama A 3-D scene that sits inside a frame

establishing shot The first shot of a new movie or a scene that shows where the action is taking place

frame One picture in a series that will be used in a movie

keyed out Removed

knead To squeeze and press

props Objects used in a play or movie

scale How large something appears in relation to something else

screening Showing a movie

sets Constructed places where movies or TV shows are filmed

storyboard A series of drawings that show the sequence of shots in a movie or TV show

story line The plan or main events of a story

top-grossing Having made the most money before deductions are taken for costs

transition A change from one place or thing to another

transparent Describes an object that can be easily seen through

tripod A three-legged stand used to hold a camera

tutorial Instructions that teach you how to use a program

INDEX